The Sky Is Bluer for One Crow

Other books by Una Nichols Hynum

Everyday Birds on Everyday Fences, 1991

Second Spring in Eden, 1996

Life Is a Found Thing, 1998

Every Dream Remembered, 1999

Tell Him Goodnight for Me, 2000

Where Summers Go, 2003

Beyond All Walking, 2005

Summer Cottage of the Heart, 2006

Cup at a Forlorn Angle, 2009

Wooden Rain, 2011

At the Foot of the Staircase, 2014

The Sky Is Bluer for One Crow

Poems
Una Nichols Hynum

BLUE VORTEX PUBLISHERS

The Sky Is Bluer for One Crow

First Edition
ISBN-13:   978-0-9726210-5-2
ISBN-10:   0-9726210-5-9
10 9 8 7 6 5 4 3 2 1

bluevortextpublishers.com
bluevortex1@yahoo.com

First paperback printing, October, 2017
Printed in the United States of America
The text in this book is composed in Palatino Linotype
Seretta Martin, Editor
Clifton King, Technical Editor
Terry Macrae, Proofreading Editor

Cover artwork: *Hesitante Spiritualite,*
Oil on Canvas by Beth Anna Otellart, Paris, France, 2015,
from her series, *"We, on the Horizon."*

BLUE VORTEX PUBLISHERS

Acknowledgments:

Some of these poems appeared in the following publications: Oasis, San Diego Poetry Annual, Ekphrasis, Serving House Journal, A Year in Ink, Southern California Haiku Anthology, City Works, and Magee Park Anthology.

Honorable Mention: *First Christmas Without You*, Steve Kowit Poetry Prize, 2016. Pushcart nominations: *The Next Poem*, Ekphrasis, 1991, and *The News*, San Diego Poetry Annual, 2015.

I would like to thank the members of Oasis, the Bluestocking Poets, Kathleen Peckham, Karen Stromberg, Oriana Ivy and Seretta Martin; my editor. Loving gratitude to daughter; Deborah Hardy, and granddaughter; Melissa Gonzalez, who made sure I got to various venues. And my special thanks to consultant and poet; Clifton King, for his expert technical guidance.

A few words of praise

There is nothing pretentious about Una's poetry. She writes about the joys, sorrows, and losses that make up the fabric of our everyday lives. But like an alchemist, she transforms the ordinary into the sublime. Her imaginative play of words, her love affair with nature, her wisdom, insight, and warmth take us to another dimension, a place of incomparable richness.

~Anne Whitlock, author of Nine Years in the Convent, A Memoir

I gauge the age
of her teapot by
how worn the handle

Table of Contents

The Sky Is Bluer for One Crow

two black cats curled
asleep on a white duvet
parenthesis

La Muneca de Isabella

Bouncy as accordion pleated paper
the doll's black curls were tied
with red ribbons, her porcelain face,
pale as a rose, fingers like a lady's
sipping tea. It was a likeness
that made Father give her the doll,
dressed as Isabella always was, in lace
starched petticoat, patent leather shoes.

Rocking in her favorite chair one day,
Isabella dropped the doll, smashing
fingers and the delicate nose.
Father said not to cry, Western Union
would know where to get her mended.

A child's calendar is a rubber band,
stretches hours into weeks but at last
a box arrived. Father pushed aside tissue paper,
lay the flawless muneca in Isabella's arms,
watched expectantly as she searched
the little face for a trace of recognition.
At last she said solemnly, *Pero, Papa,*
no me mira con los mismos ojos.
But, Papa, she does not look at me
with the same eyes.

Old Friends   *a haibun*

We walk the perimeter of the pasture
where it meets the piney woods.
The heavy odor of cows hangs in the air.
Wearing a pair of Matthew C's boots
I'm in danger of walking out of them
as we squish across the sodden field
dodging cow flops, laughing.
The sky is pewter. Clouds stagger,
threatening a gusher of summer rain.
He wants to share this little corner of the Texas
he loves, bluebonnets, blue bells, primroses
and quinine weed, to taste wild huckleberries.
We've left our spouses back at the house.
If we are in love, it doesn't occur to us to say so.
He shows me a roadside stand where he leaves
produce from his vegetable garden
with a glass jar for payment.

to leave I must break
spider silk shimmying
between the gateposts

Ah, Grasshoppers

It's always there, isn't it, this death
who's walked beside us all our lives,
keeping a low profile. Now here it is.
The doctor says inoperable cancer.
You could live a year, maybe five.

We sit, leaning into each other on the front
porch steps under that ancient evergreen
the possum calls home, remembering
how she'd come in the cat door and I'd say,
"But we don't have a white cat."

Your sister says a man has to father
a son and plant a tree before he dies.
You have two sons and the willow
is roof level and growing. It's time to tell
your friends, your family and your dog.

So here we sit, in a landslide of memories,
the past strewn around us. Suddenly
we don't want to squander a minute,
but don't know what to do with the hour.

Tumbleweeds

You don't fall in love,
you tumble
like the lacy balls
in desert wind,
bouncing across long stretches
on thorny tiptoes
until they pile up
against a fence with all
the other discarded loves.
It can happen any time,
surprises me how
often I've experienced
this crazy dance
when I touch down
only to tumble
recklessly in love again.
Tomorrow I'll tally up
how many times
I have loved and lost.
But nothing
is ever truly lost
and if I hadn't taken
a chance—
I'd grieve
for the loss of something
not experienced.
Better this dam
of prickly memories,
the promise of one more
joyous romp.

In the Wink of an Eye   *a haibun*

When willows are shaking their hips in the wind
whispering wisdom I can't quite grasp,
an original thought tries to take shape but escapes
the way stars twitch and aren't there at second glance.
Perhaps I'm not looking in the same part of the sky.
I mourn the loss of an idea, gone before I can put shoes
on it and teach it to walk, sensing I missed something
that might have saved the world or at the very least
cured cancer. I was thinking of you, giving up
both your soft young breasts.

between the shed and the willow
a flying silhouette
thought

For Beth and Victor

Beth's Wedding

The country house is a train ride from Paris,
David writes, I'm standing in the shadow of history.

The grandmother's home has been in the groom's family
for centuries, has stone walls three-feet-thick,

the fields are murmuring with bees. It's August.
David collects and presses a few unassuming wild flowers

in an envelope to bring to me, a few leaves from the arbor
he built, a piece of midnight-blue lace trimmed from the Maid

of Honor's dress. Amanda has flown in from Canada.
She wears a wreath of flowers in her new hair.

There is also a magpie feather, *one for sorrow, two for joy,*
three for a girl, four for a boy, rhyme of the magpie's feather.

My youngest granddaughter is marrying her French prince
as the air marries the light. She sends me a sprig of lavender

in a small blue bottle with a cork from the wine used
for their wedding toast. In a video the wedding party is seated

at a cloth-covered table beside the barn. David turns
on the sound. I hear laughter. And that's all: laughter. Only that.

a dog howling
in the key of sorrow
ground fog

First Christmas Without You

I keep trying to miss you, to conjure
your voice, your face.
You took part in so little all those years
no tree, no presents until the night before
when you'd send your already overburdened
adult children to look for something
when there was nothing left on the shelves.
You'd appear in time for family photos
so I know you were there.
My favorite Christmas memory is of
a candlelight service in Heidelberg, none
of the faces were familiar but the light
from the candles made them so. I wore white
sheepskin-lined boots, fur hat and mittens.
It was so silent I thought I could
hear the snowflakes falling.
You may have been there but you're
missing from my memory.

Widowhood Was Once a Rumor

After a rain the air chimes with light and wind.
There's a gaiety to everything as the last drop
traces the spear of grass, slides like a tear down

a stone face. The color of loneliness fades.
Loneliness takes two. I am a widow — I tell
the melaleuca and the weeping pepper

on my daily walk. I can say it and the word
is ambrosia on my tongue. It waited so long
to be true after years of ersatz widowhood.

Too late to be merry but not too late for
peace, for listening to the heartbeat of earth,
not too late for this lightness of being.

Annie said this is how it would be.

Horsching, Austria, 1948

Horsching was rural in the way of the Brothers Grimm,
cottages with dirt floors, a communal fountain
where hausfraus did laundry and geese chased
passersby; and next door the dismal barracks
of people displaced after the war when borders
changed and homelands no longer existed.
One day I watched a young boy from the barracks
stumble, spilling the pail of milk he was bringing
to his family. He sat down, hugged his knees,
and cried. Grabbing a bag of oranges just bought
from the commissary, I ran outside, crawled through
the barbed wire that separated us, and held them
out to him. After that he came often to weed
my herb garden and to play with my children.
I haven't written about Austria before.
It was so beautiful and I was so young,
and like the boy I could never call it home.
I didn't know this was the happiest I'd ever be.

Looking for a New Home

Fog hangs over the scramble of driftwood
like some entity bent on breaking the human spirit.

We've driven miles of Oregon coast and most days
if the sun appears it's an estranged relative

peering through a dirty windowpane.
We begin to have a creeping sense of failure.

Turning inland hoping to find a farm for sale,
more fog, drizzle, rain. Despite the dazzle of green

we feel cloistered by the dark. The slim
limb of young trees have lost their allure,

the bravado of mature trunks, no longer quaint.
At a rural café we sit at a plank table, a grey-

weathered relic, frayed as old linen. Braids
of steam rise from bowls of chowder

into the hovering cold. *Time to head back,*
he says, *You had to have been born here.*

Army Hospital, Heidelberg, Germany, 1953

It's a Boy

Pushing midnight. Soothing
womb water washes down my legs.
Good, I think, the baby's near.

An orderly tells me to lift
myself onto a gurney. Too late.
The grinding labor of birth has begun
with a furious primeval growl
I can't believe is coming from me.

The doctor catches the baby
who's not breathing,
slips a tiny oxygen mask
over his face. Like a wild thing startled
from hiding he whimpers, sampling
the air, the light.

In our room I count fingers, toes,
check penis, nuzzle the nape
of his neck, give in to the urge
to lick this child, to taste this creature,
to mark him as my own.

The Long Winter

I fold the corner of a page
to mark the place where it all began
homesick for winter that falls for days

from the heights of old age
I remember childhood's fairytale fears
I fold the corner of a page

to mark the place where ways
of the past trace my journey
wishing for winter falling for days

it began in a cottage behind a hedge
a simple slow beginning
I fold the corner of a page

to mark my place at this age
to keep close these memories
I miss winters that fell for days

life is a book I read again and again
and mark the place where it all began
I fold the corner of a page
homesick for winter that falls for days

veiled in fog
a bridge hangs ghostly
no exit

There were no covered bridges

in my New England childhood. There were stone walls and two-lane dirt roads bordered by woods, birch trees mostly, the white bark ancestors of light. White church steeples poked through them announcing the next village. Where I lived was just a stretch of road lined with mailboxes, staid as New Englanders. There were a few red barns though ours was weathered grey. It could have been the place where dreams go to die but in my case, where poems struggled to be born. Those days I delighted in everything, I harvested scraps of sorrow, sighs of defeat, tried to make sense of war and why all the boys were gone, then an occasional rainbow picked up its bright skirts and danced in its own reflection.

Culling   *a haibun*

The year I was eight my father shouldered his axe
and took me with him to the woods to pick out
a Christmas tree. That was the year I stopped
speaking to him. Everything wore a sifting of snow.
I was small so the tree I chose was modest though
to me it was magnificent and tall. He wasn't surprised
when I chose one that needed culling. He must have known
I loved all small creatures. We dragged the tree home across
frozen furrows, decorated it with strings of popcorn.
Each Christmas began like this and ended with Father
drunk at midnight, Mother and I dragging him indoors.
He didn't understand his rages had piled up like snow
against the door until it wouldn't open.

in the blue vase
every season
flowers die

Greene, Rhode Island, 1938

The Summer We Were Twelve

Summer threaded its green and golden days
through the needle of time.
That was the summer kids shed clothes,
leapt into the willow pond, surfacing
with the enthusiasm of rainbows.
Two of us splashed along the banks,
couldn't swim and that set us apart.
All the rest were from a family of sixteen.
We were shy, both only children, me in my flour sack
swim suit that became transparent when wet
so I stayed under the water up to my neck and he,
the little black boy who lived deep in the woods
and didn't attend school.
That was the summer of unencumbered glee
before time filled with tomorrows.

For my father on Father's Day

Bully

The stall reeks of fear and straw
as William cowers waiting for the whip.
He pokes straws through holes in the wall
until they bend and break.

Grandfather is a horse trader.
Grandmother boards out William as often
as she can to protect him from whippings
that over time flay pieces of the boy's spirit.

Father rarely attends school
and when he does he is too frightened to learn.
Letters and numbers wander into the trees
outside the schoolhouse window where flying

squirrels cavort from tree top to tree top
with an ease the boy admires.
Being high seems a safe place.
When William turns thirteen he's big

and strong from a childhood of hard work.
One day when Grandfather reaches
for the whip my father says quietly,
"If you ever touch me again I'll kill you."

What if…

because the whole world is recycled
plants, trees, trash, people…what if
I am reincarnated as the baby on the hill-
side in Greece overlooking the blue
Mediterranean…what if my father
is the little boy next door I play
with…kind and fun-loving…maybe I can
forgive myself for not loving him,
for not forgiving him his drunken rages.
What if we splash in the rain
play leap frog, shoot marbles,
big blue marbles like the planet earth
swirling in space…

I've Seen You Drink with the Best Irishman

You ask me how I know
if someone is an alcoholic.
I think before I answer —
fear, distaste, pity. And in your case,
sadness knowing you have the gene
that has this hold on you and nightly
drink yourself unconscious,
must muster the will to wake, shower,
find the least wrinkled shirt, grab a drink,
show up before your class, running
hands through unruly hair.
Your students unapologetically in love
with you, your teaching, your poetry.
This is not something I want to know.
I can't help you as I couldn't help my father
whose alcoholism was a looming presence
like a nest of Russian dolls. Dear teacher,
I carry the gene too.

How Many Mondays

A crow moon hangs in the sky tonight
yellow as the lye soap you used to scrub
my father's work clothes with, kneeling

in front of a slab that was once part
of the Rhode Island landscape made up
of layers of rock like our Irish cousin-country.

You were young.
I remember the legerdemain of your hands
among the suds. As you curled your arms

around the basket on the way to the clothesline
did you ever think of Eve the first morning
she realizes how many Mondays she would

spend, like you, doing a lifetime of laundry
for Adam, Cain, and the sisters, how many
Mondays she'd watch the minuet of sheets

in the wind, maybe join them in the dance.
How much sorrow can a heart hold
on a day like this, how much love.

CAUTION: Deaf Child

The whole street holds its breath.
Everything moves in slow motion,
the houses grim with responsibility,
the sidewalk, the porches.
I picture the child, islanded in silence
his hands, like the wings of small birds
in a cage, imagining them
orchestrating a meteor shower,
teaching the stars to sign.

Skip-a-Rope

Basrma is eight years old, one in the long line
of refugees that winds like a scarf, dingy, frayed
as far as she can see ahead and behind.

What is a border, she wonders. Will I remember
the name of my village that I'm told
is no longer mine, no longer wants me.

Basrma carries baby brother in a sling. Mother
balances everything they own on her head wrapped
in a bright bundle. Little brother smiles up

at Basrma, a moment of joy she doesn't believe
possible. When they stop for the night jockeying
for space somewhere on the bare ground

beside the road they travel, she hopes for a drink
of water, a bit of bread. When a falling star streaks
across the darkening sky she thinks we're scattered

like those stars. Basrma finds a piece of old rope
and with other tired children begins to skip.

Lilacs

we live as if we think we'll never die
we fear death but don't believe it
and watch the dying lilacs with a sigh

we plant our trees and in the branches tie
bright prayer rags, messages for the gods
live as if we think we'll never die

we sow our seeds flinging them wide
like peasants in old paintings
and watch the vase of lilacs with a sigh

we pluck the browning blossoms, wonder why
they can't last beyond a season, lose their smell
we want to think that we will never die

we walk to the bakery every day to buy
donuts and croissants, brew our coffee strong
and watch the wilting lilacs with a sigh

we fear death but don't believe it
death only visits those who live next door
we live as if we think we'll never die
and watch the dying lilacs with a sigh

yellow chasing yellow
across the parking lot
butterflies

I speak for the stone

the riddle wrapped in silence.
  I speak for the spark living inside
    that we see only when we strike two together.

I speak for the silvery-green lichen living on it,
  amethyst hiding in its heart,
    for slugs and sow bugs who live underneath.

When my children asked where they came from
  laughing I'd say I turned over a stone.
    I love the way a stone falls gracefully

from any height, nesting where it lays.
  I love stone walls wandering over the green hills
    of Ireland wearing tufts of wool.

I speak for the quarries and slabs of New England,
  for Frost's poison ivy covering walls that tumble
    and must be husbanded year after year like a marriage.

I speak for Stonehenge and the circles of the Isles,
  for the mystery of their stones that never tell where
    they came from, never give up the riddle of their shadows.

Ocean, I Missed You

Ocean, I missed you, she says, apple-red polished toes
clutching the edges where it creeps up the sand, spent
from its long voyage tide to tide.

Each wave catches a different sun drenching her
in memories of love-making behind the dunes, drawing
names in the sand, knowing the next wave will erase them

even before she knows she will let another love go.
Ocean, how many others feel this tug, this need to live
inside one drop of you like a melody inside a flute.

Postcard from David in Oregon

Today snow is falling in gigantic flakes.

Wind is just right around the trees

at the north edge of the fields creating

a whirlwind effect, an amazing dance

flakes slow-swirling in their fancy dresses

like a Strauss waltz. I imagine the music.

Snow is silence, falling. It's like a dream

or an old movie where so much is happening

without sound. I'm a poet without words.

The brokenness of the world is heavy.

And my heart is full of slamming doors.

Where the deer stood

on the road in wet dawn light
like my face in a steamy mirror
mysterious, lonely, climbing
out of a dream. I wanted to rub a circle.
Her eyes shivered like candle flames
innocent, curious,
before she crossed to a meadow,
blended into the shoulder of a shadow
the hollow echo of her dainty hooves
clicking on the mountain road.

I Take Note

Good Morning, Morning,
oh my, you're not dressed —

naked blue, no scattered
lingerie of clouds. In my

pajamas I sit on the porch,
curly steam from my coffee

climbs the chill. Crumbling
graham crackers for jays

and squirrels, I notice a hawk
silhouetted on an antenna.

Hawk hunts with her eyes
as I try to pour you

into my cupped hands, swallow
you to prime my thirst for life

but you run through my fingers
as every morning does.

Thistle Butterflies

A field cross-stitched with wild mustard and daisies,
beside the estuary, has attracted migrating painted
ladies. The fanning of thousands, some say millions
of wings, and the fields seem to breathe.

Enchanted by this fluttering flood, this almost-touch
of wings, I hold my face up the way I greet rain. I'm
wearing a coat of butterflies. It reminds me of when
my mother held a paper pattern up to measure me

before cutting the cloth. This churning confusion
of wings among the butterflies turns my raw, restless
thoughts to battlefields, terrorism, mutilated bodies,
while I, on my safe little acre, am untouched.

Cloud Pocket

The sky is birthday-party blue,

small, playful clouds chase

each other like white train cars.

They never catch up.

One cloud wears another cloud

like a deep gray pocket.

What would I put in a cloud pocket

knowing how soon it will melt

into nothingness like spun sugar.

I'd fold myself into the lint

at the bottom like a cat, eyes closed

paws tucked, ready to purr.

Maybe I'd bring an armchair

to curl up with the ever-present

book that falls when I doze, surprising me.

Probably this is how I'll die

under the weight of Moby Dick

or Rilke's Sonnets to Orpheus.

His Master's Voice

You live most of your life
with your voice tucked inside
like a joey in a pouch.

Remember hearing it
for the first time. Perhaps
on a recording your son makes

of you reading poetry.
That can't be me—inside you hear
a bitter-chocolate-brown voice

and discover it's melting
whipped cream. No wonder people
ask, *Is your mother home?*

Humbled, aghast, what to do.
Changing will be like divorcing
the wind. Instead you strive

to lower the range the way one
changes the key on the piano,
You want it to be not exactly your voice

— but not exactly not.

vintage handkerchief
one corner wears a knot of string
parachute

At the foot of the staircase

the stairs land in infinity
rise to the attic where histories are stored
dressmaker's dummy, butter churn, a sextant—
past the room of crazy great grandmother
keep going out the window sweeping up
through the thinnest stars—the hooked moon
curved around its coming phase, barely visible,
a sonogram unveiling the complexities it will
be born with—what small changes can we see
from earth when in our back yard buds appear
on the willow, young-green leaves on the dormant
fig, paint begins to peel from the north side
of the house—tread by tread the stairs come back,
faithfully returning the day—crazy granny
throws a teacup from her barred window
a scattering of porcelain petals on the walk.

threat

dark thins into light like pouring milk
into black tea, clouds have stretch marks,
day comes light as a cat, lovely in its
seeming harmlessness but the room's
soft air is full of menace,
even the desk that looks so static is shuffling
atoms and nuzzling notebooks, something
in the drawer crashes, tendrils of bindweed
claw their way under the door

life is a learning experience and most of us
never learn, we aren't even paper trained
and need to have our noses rubbed
in whatever, forever, the threat of wars,
revolutions, genocide — a cobweb of thought, frail
as a dream, when will peace be the world's
weapon of choice, when will we stop
thundering through history
stomping on poppies and newborn grass.

Mosaic

Seven gables, six chimneys, one outhouse,
a linen closet, little fort among the baskets,
a bed pushed against a wall, peeling strips of pink
flowered wall paper tucked under the mattress,
dreaming of a snake that only wanted to talk,
wearing a heavy grey turtleneck at the zoo
watching Galapagos tortoises mating, church bells
chiming, pealing, muffled, black quarantine sign
on the door, autumn, season of falling apart, leaves
burning, spring, a little stream, shallow, every pebble
mirror-clear, small hands captivated by wild flowers
learning their language, brailing early melancholy
on the sand, picnic, salmon sandwiches, baby lettuce
from gran's garden, donut holes with powdered
sugar and nutmeg, Santa Ana winds, soft, warm, all
windows open, curtains blowing over the sill, a paper
swallow swinging on a thread.

If You're Smoking in This House You'd Better Be on Fire

I can't bear to put smoke rings in my poems
or inch thick crystal ash trays, no music box
playing *The Beautiful Blue Danube*
as compartments open, offering cigarettes.

My mother smokes and my Dad (I gave him cartoons
of cigarettes for Christmas, helped him roll his own).
My husband smoked and all our friends.
I wore a married smile, watched the white
paisley curling on the ceiling.

When I was in school the girls began
to smoke thinking it made them glamorous
like movie stars. My first date said
I'd look sophisticated holding a cigarette.

I said no. Not "Goody Two-Shoes," just fed
up without knowing why. Now, my husband's
caregiver, I watch the slow, slow death by
coughing, gagging, spitting, gasping.

Thanks, Bette Davis and Paul Henreid,
blowing your seductive smoke rings into the dark.

Now Is a Good Time to Be Crazy

Everyone goes down the street

talking to themselves, waving

their arm, in deep conversation

with a shiny black beetle in their ear.

No one will notice you singing, preaching

to the air, grass and concrete.

You can recite poetry to store windows.

No one cares. Carry a broken umbrella,

do a dance step or two. You can get away

with anything. Everyone wears

that vacant-lot look, so go ahead

turn your imaginary apron into a basket

and gather your imaginary pears.

Meditation

No amount of "ooohming" keeps
me concentrated on the breath.
Thoughts bleed around the edges
of "ooohm" like light around an eclipse
of the moon.
Thoughts play connect the dots—a shoe
wagging a foot—a ragged shirt
turkey dinner at the Salvation Army,
Dad's home grown turkeys,
Sunday chicken dinners—blood
picking pin feathers, on and on.
One potato, Two potato, another
slippage of thought.
I haven't taken a deep breath for so long
I've forgotten what I'm listening for.

Sleep

...is a little maid
in a dust cap with a broom
who does housekeeping
in the mind, deep cleaning,
sweeps cobwebs, mops up spills,
finds lost keys, chops down stinging nettles,
locates answers to questions,
scribbled on slips of pink post-its,
often losing the answers.
Occasionally she sits and sips
tea, watches the dregs of past wander by,
cogitates what else needs to be done
before day straggles over the horizon.
And we wake surprised, feeling cleansed.
But sometimes when the little maid
wrings out her mop of dreams
she spills sadness and we wake,
our cheeks wet with tears.

Smiling Buddha in an Old Museum

When sweaty hands rub my fat belly for luck
I wish them well. My smile is contagious,

strained through the sieve of centuries, so even
when visitors make fun of me they can't help

smiling. Sometimes I pretend to turn
my massive backside like the gorilla in the zoo.

Sometimes I time-travel—Kyoto, Edo, the Isle of Skye,
my atoms busier than dust in a sunbeam.

The hardest part of smiling for hundreds of years
is—seeing the young who touch my belly without hope.

With Thanks to Lucille Clifton~

Someone had to tell me, had to say out loud

"the American language is beautiful,"

and I saw it right away. Someone had to tell me

how all the languages of the world

washed up on our shore with a rich potage of words:

"billabong, dingo, banshee, shillelagh, wee

and canny, concierge, aubergine, loch and crag,

apartheid, spoor, chutzpah, oy vey…"

For years I envied the seductive purr of French,

the vivacity of Italian, breathless Chinese,

German, so stout and Russian so sure of itself.

Someone has to tell me my own language is beautiful

before I notice how many words sidle up, make way

for rhyme, with so little effort on my part,

how at ease with themselves and each other.

Librarians

Scent of old books and glue, essence
of language, and I think of all the librarians
sitting behind their desks who stamped
my treasured card allowing me entrance
to the shelves of silence where knowledge
sprouted among diaries, poetry and mysteries.

I grew up among the curators of silence
who hushed us when there was giggling
in the stacks. Shadowy, nameless librarians.
I wish I could go back and hug the only one
I recall at all, her prim little body, put a smile
on her lips, pursed from years of shushing.

Because of her I was kidnapped by history
and geography, learned to travel the world
with a roll of the globe, a flip through the card catalog.
And I don't even remember her name.
I'd like to cross the country by back roads,

stop in little villages, find the libraries,
hug the librarians, leave a thank you note,
a poem that when unsealed, a cascade
of tiny angels will tumble out
and ask for his or her name.

When I can't sleep

my mind goes island hopping along an archipelago of thoughts from little things like the dryer eating Jacob's knitted helmet with earflaps to world peace to the fall of the Berlin Wall. This drowsy state of memory doesn't distinguish between past, present and future. I stand again on that balcony at Konstanzerstrasse airing feather bedding with my German neighbors or I spend an afternoon at the Louvre admiring the Mona Lisa and Winged Victory. Most of my islands are forested with worries that take up residence, playing over and over as if rehearsing a song I dislike—bedfellows of bad memories. Get out of my thoughts. I don't want to feel less of a person because parallel parking and computers are beyond me. Get off my islands. Let a profusion of lush beauty cover them. Let sleep come—a spinnaker slowly filling with wind.

Poet

This morning I'm taking a verb for a walk—
prevaricate. A poet friend and I discussed how long
it's been since we heard the word used or *indubitably*
or felonious. Decided this generation speaks in clichés,
slang, acronyms and profanity, nothing over two syllables.

As a child I collected words like shells and stones
stored them on the shelf of my mind, copied them
crudely into a notebook. I read Hawthorne's
House of Seven Gables with a dictionary at my elbow
determined to learn a better vocabulary.

As a poet I fall in love with language every day
skipping with rhyme and rhythm, stitching and unstitching
them into the seam of a poem, knowing that with every
sentence I preserve Latin, Greek and Anglo Saxon
weaving them into the music of daily speech.

in the nursing home
Jim calls *is anybody there*
Anybody

The Edge

Pieces of earth break loose
and tumble from a cliff posted "unstable."
I listen for the thud on the beach far below.

Standing at a different edge,
I'm already thinking of what I'll miss,
things I won't know I'm missing:

mud puddles drying after rain, cracked
like shaved chocolate, a moon breaking free
of the mountain, a watercolor of the moon.

I'll miss the feline beauty of fog
the shabby chic of empty nests,
the way the world sleeps;

Baby Jacob on the kitchen floor
sitting in the non-stick frying pan
grinning like Buddha.

The voice of the waves is rising.
Every day I'm one step closer to the edge.
In the trembling of a moment I already
miss the last poem I might have written.

Rehearsal

Once upon a time
there was a tree.
I sat in its shade every day,

an angel's trumpet
with hundreds of massive cream blossoms
hanging like prayer rags.

Today it fell
in a heap like a discarded prom dress.
A week ago I sat across the street

and sketched it
hoping to do a painting.
The sky is incomplete without it.

Death will come like this
on a day like any other.
There was no wind.

Aunt Betty

I don't have time for dying, leaving
these glorious sunsets and even small
things like that trail of ants and I have
yet to coax a butterfly to sit on my hand.

My bucket list has a thousand things
not checked off: another train ride (upper
deck, please) another walk on a lonely beach,
one more snowy day with paw prints,

another love affair, not to mention Paris.
And I haven't had time to master French.
When we were young we hurried past
these woods. What were we afraid of? Death

was a distant relative we heard about and hoped
when she visited she wouldn't be as testy
as we'd heard. You know, I don't even
have the address of where I'm going.

Frankenstein's Monster

Even the stars wince at the sight of me,
a derelict made up of cadaver parts stitched together,
a soul, do I have one or was it left out
without language until I listen through
a hole in the wall as a young woman teaches
her cousin to read unfolding the fan of my days,
thoughts coming like heat lightning
there is a love in me the likes of which you have never seen,
there is a rage in me the likes of which you will never believe.
I wander the Arctic looking not for what was lost
but for what I never had.
I kill what my creator loved,
he was my father,
he never gave me a name.

Soliloquy

I hold my skull in both hands, feel cheekbones, jawbone,
eye socket, brows, the bump from my last fall.
The skull is solid, tactile like a woodcut.
I think of the graveyard scene in Hamlet.
The gravedigger unearths a skull polished by time,
a bit muddied, and Hamlet says, "Alas, Poor Yorick,
I knew him," and recalls how the jester carried him piggyback
"a thousand times." No one will say, "Alas Poor Una,
I knew her." All will be ashes. The skull will be last to burn.
Thought was housed there but wasn't the brain
only the vessel for thought? Where did my words
and voice really come from?
The soul does not succumb to fire so where does it go
when the rest of its house goes up in flame?

The Next Poem

The next poem I write will have a saxophone in it
golden neck catching theater lights, ripping up the backdrop
like heat lightning and a range that stuns. I'll have to wear
cotton in my ears. The next poem
will have the sea in it and a long stretch
of sandy beach, a flock of small sand pipers lifting off
like notes from the score of a Puccini opera, twisted
silver and gold in the sun. The next poem
will have a music box made of mahogany with sandalwood.
It will play "The Faust Waltz," doors will open and there
will be *everlasting* in all the cubby holes.
There will be a conductor in the next poem with a gold baton.
Oh, there will be slivers of music in the next poem
and shards of melody.

The News

The rain has stopped. I wake to the slap
of tires on the wet street and a hawk's hunting
cry down by the river. Today I want to bandage
the whole world, but no matter how thick
the gauze of words, blood leaks through,
leaving behind a trail like a failed abortion.
Outside on the pavement a newspaper, soaked
with rain, opens its mouth to speak, then closes.

The Orchard Within

The cold seeps into bricks and beams.

All the hidden spaces resist the heater's

efforts to warm my yesterdays.

Up to my chin in cold despite quilts

and blankets I dream of the tender-warm

shadows of summer, the peach orchard

I carry within me. The book I'm reading

reaches out from its pages. The main

character has fallen in love with me.

Bless the hot soup he brings to page 31,

and the remaining 200 pages

he sprinkles with buttercups.

Walking among the Cabbages*

Supposing I wished this fire on myself
by thinking about the Buddhist admonition
to get rid of *things*. What would happen,
I thought, if I were empty, what would it be like
to start over. The universe has big ears.

Supposing the dream of living like Basho—
walking stick, begging bowl, a not-too-clean
cloak, poetry—what if this dream brought
on the loss of home, olive tree and fig,
paper lanterns.

Supposing this is a tragedy, not an adventure.
But no one is shooting at me. I haven't lost
a homeland or family. What if this sickly calm
among the black ruins is about, *'Who am I.'*
What if the moon can't find its way back
to my window.

*…"dawn, walking among the cabbages…
~17th century dictionary

The Sky Is Bluer for One Crow

Now I am old, looking more like my great grandmother
every day, wizened, squinty eyed, let me view the world
through a kaleidoscope, flipping from hyacinth to aubergine
to sunset pinks to night coated in moonlight.

Let me see the world out of whack. Let it hurt.

I want to be quaint like the little towns I promised to come
back to as they receded in the rear view mirror when I drove
away, houses with a profusion of wisteria behind picket fences,
everything warm as stones after a day in the sun.

Let me think like a mountain. Let me mourn.

Now I am old, I want poetry to come looking for me.
I want to be bewitched by words, to bedevil the evil I see.
Let me unlace the wrongs I've done. Let me forgive myself.
Let the sky be bluer for my passing through.

About the Author

Former United States Poet Laurate, Billy Collins once called Una Nichols Hynum, "the poet who made me wake up." Una is the author of twelve books of poetry and a finalist for the James Hearst Poetry Prize, Margie and Writers Digest. She has been nominated for the Pushcart. Una is a member of the Squaw Valley Community of Writers and her poetry has appeared in in *Rattle, an island of egrets, A Year in Ink, San Diego Poetry Annual, Magee Park Anthology, Oasis Journal, Synesthesia Literary Journal, Cider Press Review, Serving House Journal, Ekphrasis, The Reader,* and numerous other anthologies. She feels privileged to have worked with many of the best poets of San Diego including her mentor, Steve Kowit. Una holds a BA degree from San Diego State University.

BLUE VORTEX PUBLISHERS

www.ingramcontent.com/pod-product-compliance
Lightning Source LLC
Chambersburg PA
CBHW072231170526
45158CB00002BA/851